Gifts of Her Spirit

poems by

Sister Mary Brigh Cassidy

MAYO CLINIC PRESS

The material for this book was prepared by Sister Lauren Weinandt and Jane K. Campion, friends of Sister Mary Brigh, who have protected Sister's writing and believe the gift of her poetry should be shared.

Published by Mayo Clinic Press

Copyright © 2021 Mayo Foundation for Medical Education and Research

For bulk sales to employers, member groups, and health-related companies, contact Mayo Clinic, 200 First St. SW, Rochester, MN 55905, call 800-430-9699, or send an email to SpecialSalesMayoBooks@mayo.edu.

ISBN: 978-1-893005-75-4

Library of Congress Cataloging-in-Publication Data: 2021939737

Photographs of Sister Mary Brigh and Saint Marys Hospital are courtesy of the Saint Marys Hospital archives. Cover illustration by John W. Desley and James E. Rownd.

We believe Sister Mary Brigh Cassidy would dedicate her poetry to her parents and sisters whose deep faith steeped her life in the Gospel and the Eucharist; her Sisters in the Franciscan Community who shared her faithfulness to the Franciscan Charism; and every person who serves in the healing mission of Jesus at Saint Marys Hospital and Mayo Clinic.

—Sister Lauren Weinandt, O.S.F.,
   and Jane K. Campion

Acknowledgements

*G*ifts of Her Spirit was made possible with the help of Saint Marys Hospital Auxiliary Volunteers, who so generously supported and funded this publication; Sister Alice Thraen, O.S.F., and Sister Mary Pat Smith, O.S.F., who first typed Sister Mary Brigh's poetry; and Sister Mary Brigh's religious community, the Sisters of Saint Francis, Academy of Our Lady of Lourdes, for their support of this publication.

The 2021 edition of *Gifts of Her Spirit* was made possible through a collaboration of the Sisters of Saint Francis and Mayo Clinic. Sister Lauren Weinandt, O.S.F., proposed a reprinted edition and supported the project with co-editor Jane Campion. Sister Ramona Miller, O.S.F., congregational minister/president, and Michael Speltz, treasurer, approved the project on behalf of the leadership of the Sisters of Saint Francis. Matthew Dacy and Jeanne Klein provided support and project administration through Mayo Clinic Heritage Days. Michael Cleary, Media Support Services, took photographs in Saint Marys Chapel and the hospital. Mayo Clinic Press provided additional editorial and design support.

Sister Mary Brigh Cassidy

Poems

 Advent and Christmas

 *Lent and Easter*

 Ordinary Time

Welcome

On behalf of the Sisters of Saint Francis, it is an honor to present this new edition of *Gifts of Her Spirit: Poems by Sister Mary Brigh Cassidy.*

Since its first publication in 2008, *Gifts of Her Spirit* has been warmly received by people from many places and walks of life. We recognize with gratitude Sister Lauren Weinandt and Jane Campion, longtime friends and colleagues of Sister Mary Brigh, who co-edited the volume of her poetry; Sister Tierney Trueman, who wrote the introduction; Marianne Hockema, author of the foreword; Virginia Woodruff, who shared creative skills as typographer; the Saint Marys Hospital archives, which provided historic images; and Artpacks, which provided additional photographs and artwork. Their collaboration made the 2008 edition possible with generous support from the Saint Marys Hospital Auxiliary Volunteers.

In 2021, The Academy of Our Lady of Lourdes transferred copyright of *Gifts of Her Spirit* to Mayo Foundation for Medical Education and Research. We express appreciation to Mayo Clinic Press and Mayo Clinic Heritage Days for making this edition possible. Here, you will find original content from

Gifts of Her Spirit. This edition also provides an essay on the "handshake" that symbolizes the collaboration between the Franciscan Sisters and Mayo Clinic, placing the poetry of Sister Mary Brigh into historical context.

As in the first edition, Sister Mary Brigh's poems are arranged according to the Liturgical Year of the Catholic Church. This calendar served as the prism for Sister Mary Brigh's writing. Note the symbols that mark different sections of the book. They are inspired by images from Saint Marys Chapel and hospital. Sister Lauren explains they are printed on each page approximately where readers place their thumbs while holding the book—providing a unique, tactile connection to the mission of Saint Marys and Mayo Clinic. Use of gray in the design also is intentional. Jane Campion shares that Sister Mary Brigh was not a black-and-white person. As befitting a poet, she appreciated "shades of gray" and nuance within the construct of her faith.

Among many poems that are included here, one of my favorites is "Change." Its admonition, "Change is inexorable," resonates today. At the same time, we can face the future with confidence through the grace-filled insights of Sister Mary Brigh Cassidy, which are in truth the gifts of her spirit.

—Sister Ramona Miller, O.S.F.

   Congregational Minister / President
   Sisters of Saint Francis
   Rochester, Minnesota

The Handshake

Sister Mary Brigh Cassidy wrote poetry that expresses her own life experience. Her poems also speak to the values of her religious community, the Sisters of Saint Francis—inspired, dedicated, tenacious and remarkable women—and their collaboration with Mayo Clinic. This collaboration is symbolized in the simple but powerful gesture of a handshake.

It began before Sister Mary Brigh's administrative leadership of Saint Marys Hospital from 1949 to 1971 and it continues today. One could think of the larger Mayo-Franciscan relationship as bookends to the poems in *Gifts of Her Spirit.*

The collaboration took root in crisis. On August 21, 1883, a tornado devasted the prairie town of Rochester, Minnesota. William Worrall Mayo, M.D., an immigrant from England who had been in Rochester for nineteen years, was placed in charge of helping the injured survivors. He needed assistance and turned to Mother Alfred Moes, an immigrant from Luxembourg and founder of the Sisters of Saint Francis, who had established a school in Rochester six years before.

The Sisters were teachers, but they met the challenge and worked with Dr. Mayo and his sons, William J. Mayo, M.D., who was barely three months out of medical school, and Charles H. Mayo, who would start medical school two years later. The Mayos, the Sisters, and others who joined them provided emergency care in makeshift facilities, including a library and a dance hall.

When the crisis had passed, Mother Alfred called upon Dr. W. W. Mayo. She described a bold plan: The Sisters would raise funds to build a hospital and serve as nurses if he and his sons would provide the medical and surgical services.

Dr. Mayo resisted. It was an expensive, risky idea ... further, many patients in that era shunned hospitals as dirty and dangerous, where the poor and ill, with no one to care for them, went to die.

Mother Alfred persisted. She envisioned a hospital where Dr. Mayo's strong, intelligent sons and her meticulous, dedicated Sisters could provide a new type of care. "With our faith and hope and energy," she assured him, "it will succeed."

The next moment in their conversation was the hinge of history at Mayo Clinic. Dr. Mayo accepted Mother Alfred's offer. Saint Marys Hospital opened in 1889 and played a key role in transforming Dr. Mayo's family practice into an internationally acclaimed medical center. As Cokie Roberts, award-winning journalist and member of the Mayo Clinic Board of Trustees, said: "If it hadn't been for a pushy nun who wouldn't take 'No' for an answer, Saint Marys Hospital would have never been built, and what became known as Mayo Clinic might not have ever existed."

Dr. Mayo was a man of science who admired Charles Darwin. Mother Alfred was a woman of faith who placed her congregation under the sponsorship of Our Lady of Lourdes. They had a shared commitment to serve patients and advance medical science. What they never had was a legal contract.

Literally or figuratively, their "handshake" initiated more than a century of Mayo-Franciscan collaboration.

From the start, it was inclusive of all. The question arose as to whether Saint Marys was intended for Catholic patients only. Mother Alfred would have none of it: "The cause of suffering humanity knows no religion and no sex; the charity of the Sisters of Saint Francis is as broad as their religion." Dr. Mayo's son, William J. Mayo, M.D., continued this theme in a declaration that ran counter to the culture of segregation that prevailed at the time: "… all classes of people, the poor as well as the rich, without regard to color or creed, shall be cared for without discrimination."

Mutual respect fostered teamwork and innovation. Saint Marys was among the first hospitals in the United States to adopt antiseptic methods—which meant that the Mayo brothers and the Franciscan Sisters were soon reporting high volumes of complex surgical procedures with excellent outcomes. Colleagues with diverse, complementary skills joined them, creating the model of multispecialty group practice. Rochester, Minnesota, became a beacon for patients and medical professionals alike. "The group," as Dr. Will Mayo described them, developed an ethos of service and excellence, which evolved into the three-fold mission of patient care, medical research, and medical education. Saint Marys established a school of nursing from which Julia Cassidy, later Sister Mary Brigh Cassidy when she made her religious vows, graduated in 1928.

From the start, Saint Marys was owned, led, and staffed by Franciscan Sisters and was legally separate from Mayo Clinic, which was an outpatient practice. Bonds of mutual trust connected the two organizations. Saint Marys relied upon Mayo Clinic for patients and physicians to treat them; Mayo Clinic relied upon the hospital services and staff that Saint Marys provided.

Mayo Clinic had a similar arrangement with other hospitals in downtown Rochester, managed by the Kahler Corporation and, after World War II, with Rochester Methodist Hospital.

Following Mother Alfred, Sister Joseph Dempsey served as superintendent of Saint Marys from 1892 to 1939. Her death, within a few months of both Mayo brothers in 1939, proved the strength of the Mayo-Franciscan "handshake." Leaders had carefully groomed their successors—in fact, the years of greatest expansion came after the founders had passed.

Sister Domitilla DuRocher served as administrator of Saint Marys from 1939 to 1949. She captured its distinctive character: "How does a Sisters' hospital differ from other hospitals? The chief differences are due to the fact that a Sisters' hospital is their home ... that fact affects hospital construction, organization, and hospital administration."

By the time Sister Mary Brigh Cassidy became administrator in 1949, Saint Marys was one of the largest private hospitals in the world. Until her retirement in 1971, she led Saint Marys through unparalleled growth. Milestones during her leadership included the Nobel Prize-winning discovery and clinical application of cortisone, pioneering work in open-heart surgery, and development of the Intensive Care Unit. She also faced unprecedented challenges in the polio epidemics of the 1950s and the Second Vatican Council of the Catholic Church, which affected the staffing and governance of Saint Marys Hospital.

To each encounter, Sister Mary Brigh brought the soul of a poet and the acumen of a business executive. When negotiating with her Mayo Clinic counterparts—most of them men and few of them Catholic—she demonstrated "quiet Irish chutzpah," in the words of one observer. Her own hard-earned perspective was "I have often thought, and sometimes said, I would hate to be a hospital administrator if I did not believe in God."

Through it all, Sister Mary Brigh was grounded in the hospital's mission: "Saint Marys became part of me ... . Particularly, I never lost touch with its spirit of dedicated service to the sick, the desire to give the best that could be given with what was then available and to seek ways to make better ... cures possible in the future."

In a seamless transition, Sister Mary Brigh was succeeded by her assistant administrator, Sister Generose Gervais, who led Saint Marys from 1971 to 1986, and until her death in 2016 served as president of the Poverello Foundation, which provides financial support to patients at Saint Marys with financial need. Sister Generose "was as comfortable with the complexity of blueprints as she was canning fruit," said one colleague. Many co-workers were quick to quote Sister Generose, who often said "No money, no mission." She readily reminded them, however, of the corollary: "No mission, no need for money."

The "handshake" assumed new dimensions in 1986, when Mayo Clinic established joint governance with Saint Marys Hospital and Rochester Methodist Hospital, uniting three separate organizations into one corporate entity. In 2014, the hospitals achieved joint licensure and are now known as Mayo Clinic Hospital-Rochester: a single hospital with two distinct campuses, the Saint Marys Campus and the Methodist Campus. Five buildings on the Saint Marys Campus are named for the Sisters who served as administrators of the hospital: Mother Alfred, Sister Joseph, Sister Domitilla, Sister Mary Brigh, and Sister Generose. The Francis Building recognizes all the Franciscan Sisters who have lived, worked, and served at Saint Marys.

In recent years, key attributes of the Mayo-Franciscan "handshake" have been articulated as Mayo Clinic Values: respect, integrity, compassion, healing, teamwork, innovation, excellence, and stewardship. Today, the Mayo Clinic Values Council provides leadership in perpetuating the Franciscan legacy and the Mayo Clinic Values across all of Mayo Clinic.

"We know who we are with the Sisters. We don't know what we would be without them," explained W. Eugene Mayberry, M.D., the Mayo Clinic chief executive whose career overlapped with Sister Mary Brigh. In the introduction to *The Little Book of Mayo Clinic Values: A Field Guide for Your Journey,* Gianrico Farrugia, M.D., president and CEO of Mayo Clinic, wrote: "Enduring values inspire dynamic innovation. This enables us to evolve with purpose." Ken Burns, producer of the documentary film *The Mayo Clinic: Faith-Hope-Science,* said: "I can think of no story more quintessentially American than that of Mayo Clinic ... . Ultimately, it addresses the age-old question of what we owe each other in terms of how we care for one another. This quest was the original animating spirit of Mother Alfred, W. W. Mayo and Mayo's sons. And it's still practiced there today."

In this book, although she might demur, the final word is best left to Sister Mary Brigh Cassidy, who expressed her own spirit as well as that of her congregation and the hospital they cherish within the mission of Mayo Clinic:

> *"It is often almost, but it never really is*
> *tomorrow. It is always only today. We have*
> *only today in which to work, to pray, to dream,*
> *to plan and to help build a better world."*

—Matthew D. Dacy
  Chair, Mayo Clinic Heritage Days

Introduction

Who was she—this woman from whose heart flowed musical words of many notes that wove the interludes of her life into one magnificent symphony of love for her God and all of Creation?

Sister Mary Brigh was a woman of great vision and wisdom. She recognized the gifts God had given her and used them to affirm and empower others. Her life might be best understood through the words of her poems. Her feet were ever grounded in her humble acceptance of who she was—a child of God. "My soul doth magnify the Lord—Who called me all unbidden in my youth to be His own, Who led me in His way." Sister Mary Brigh moved through her whole life being a sister to others, status blind, as one of her Sisters described her. She visited patients on a daily basis and brought their lives into her prayers, "Have pity, Lord, on all within these walls who toss in pain." Her door was always open to anyone who wished to enter—"A lady fair of high estate, with smiles alike for poor and great." All these fragments were part of her symphony—"Trusting that when they're gathered all together, the odds and ends that make this life of mine, Your touch will weld them into one clear pattern and find a place for them in heaven's design."

Her life was a poem-prayer of gratitude to God for "days of hard work and the quiet that evening brings ... home, loved ones, friends who support us always, and staunch faith in God." Her trust in God's love for her never faltered. Even as the illness that came to her in the twilight hours of her life dimmed her awareness of reality, her heart never ceased praying— "Though Your Footsteps lead me on dark pathways, and Your service brings battles and scars, I'll falter not, but follow to the end, my King."

—Sister Tierney Trueman, O.S.F.
   Community Minister
   Sisters of Saint Francis, Rochester, Minnesota

Statue of the Blessed Virgin Mary that was on the portico of the
main entrance of Saint Marys Hospital in 1908

Foreword

Julia Cassidy's love of nature was inevitable. Her childhood was spent on a small farm nestled between rolling green hills and dense woods in southeastern Minnesota. Even as a young girl, Julia was attuned to the rhythm of the changing seasons—each with its own purpose, challenges, and rewards. Those seasons provided a sense of order and the framework for all her family's activities.

Her aptitude for writing may have been inevitable, as well. Her mother was a voracious reader and writer of poetry and often encouraged young Julia to capture her thoughts in writing, too. Julia's first job was that of page editor and "cub reporter" for the local newspaper.

Her older sister encouraged her to consider a career in nursing, so Julia gave up her newspaper "beat" and enrolled in the Saint Marys School of Nursing. Later in life, she would recall hearing a call from God during her schooling, but she put it aside.

A second call, louder and more persistent, came when she was caring for a woman in Chicago whose home had no heat and whose cupboards were empty.

"I did not say 'no' a second time," she recounted. She entered the convent in 1935 to become a Franciscan Sister at age 29 and from that day, was known as Sister Mary Brigh. A religious counselor at the time told her that with her age and experience, he didn't know if she would be a better Sister or worse, but that she would be different—and indeed, she was.

Throughout her fifty-five-year career at Saint Marys Hospital, Sister Mary Brigh remained a common person with uncommon capabilities. To whatever position she held, she brought a business acumen that was legendary, though she was quick to dismiss her extraordinary gifts for leadership as ordinary. She approached problems quietly, yet in her calmness was a steely resolve. To those closest to her, she shared a droll sense of humor, tinged at times with a bit of whimsy. Above all, she had a deep and abiding love for Saint Marys Hospital, its patients and staff. She simply said, "Saint Marys became part of me."

In truth, it was Sister Mary Brigh who for many years was recognized as the face of Saint Marys by patients, staff, and the community. She organized, she administered, she planned, she built, she taught, and she counseled. And at the end of every long and challenging day she walked through the halls of Saint Marys, personally visiting patients from all walks of life and encouraging staff.

She continued to write poetry throughout her life, often using images from nature to capture the beauty and poignancy found in the seasons of the church and in the seasons of life.

For those who knew Sister Mary Brigh Cassidy, her life itself was a gift of the Spirit. For those who read these poems, the wonder of that gift is revealed through her words.

—Marianne L. Hockema
  Administrator, Mayo Clinic, Rochester, Minnesota

Chronology

and

Photographic Narrative

Chronology

Biographical Notes

Sister Mary Brigh Cassidy, O.S.F., R.N.

Born 1906 in Eyota, Minnesota.

Member of Third Order Regular of Saint Francis of the Congregation of Our Lady of Lourdes, 1935–1992.

Education

Graduate of Saint Marys School of Nursing, Rochester, Minnesota, 1928.

B.S. in Nursing Education, College of Saint Teresa, Winona, Minnesota, 1940.

M.S. in Nursing Education, Catholic University, Washington D.C., 1942.

M.B.A. in Hospital Administration, University of Chicago, Chicago, Illinois, 1949.

Positions at Saint Marys Hospital, Rochester, Minnesota

Night Supervisor, 1934–1935.

Instructor, Saint Marys School of Nursing, 1939–1945.

Personnel Director, 1945–1948.

Administrative Assistant, June-December 1949.

Hospital Administrator, 1949–1971.

Consultant to Administration, 1972.

Committee and Board Membership

President of the Catholic Hospital Association, 1967–1968.

President of the Minnesota Hospital Association, 1968–1969.

Member of the House of Delegates, American Hospital Association, 1971–1974.

Member of Council on Administrative Practice and the Council on Professional Practice of the American Hospital Association.

Past President and member of the Board of Minnesota Conference of Catholic Hospitals.

Fellow in the American College of Hospital Administrators.

Member of Priorities Committee, Total Community Development, Rochester, Minnesota.

Member of Committee to Study National Health Plan of the American Hospital Association.

Member of Board of Trustees, Saint Marys Hospital, 1969.

Member of Board of Trustees, College of Saint Teresa, Winona, Minnesota, 1966–1975.

Member of Board of Trustees, Mercy Hospital, Portsmouth, Ohio, 1972, 1974, 1975.

Member of Board of Trustees, Samaritan Bethany Home, Rochester, Minnesota, 1972–1978.

Member of Advisory Committee, Rochester Better Chance, 1974–1979.

Council Member of the Congregation of Our Lady of Lourdes.

Awards

Teresa of Avila Award from the College of Saint Teresa, Winona, Minnesota in 1960.

Golden Doorknob Award from the Rochester Business and Professional Women in 1969.

Woman of Achievement Award from the Minnesota Federation of Business and Professional Women's Club in 1970.

Benemerenti Papal Award in 1971.

*Sister Mary Brigh Cassidy
was born Julia Teresa Cassidy
on February 19, 1906 in Eyota,
about fifteen miles east of
Rochester, Minnesota.*

Julia Teresa Cassidy in 1918 at age 12

Julia played basketball
in high school.

Standing at right with the Eyota High School basketball team, 1920s

She graduated from high school in 1925.

Julia Teresa Cassidy as a young woman

Julia Cassidy came to Rochester to study nursing at Saint Marys School of Nursing. This was the beginning of a career at Saint Marys Hospital where she lived, worked, and served for fifty-five years; first as a nurse, then as a teacher and administrator.

Saint Marys Hospital, 1941

In 1928,
Julia Teresa Cassidy
graduated from Saint Marys
School of Nursing.

Julia Teresa Cassidy, 1928

*She entered the gospel life as a Sister
of Saint Francis in Rochester,
Minnesota, in 1935 and became known as
Sister Mary Brigh Cassidy.*

*With a steadfast focus on patient care, during her
tenure as administrator, Saint Marys Hospital
undertook two major building projects, the
Domitilla Building in 1956 and the Alfred Building
in 1967, as well as an addition to Marian Hall.*

*Sister Mary Brigh organized the personnel
department at the hospital, the health service
for employees, and the Saint Marys Hospital
Auxiliary Volunteers.*

Sister Mary Brigh Cassidy, 1963

In 1980, the Mary Brigh Building, a $55.5 million addition to Saint Marys, was named in honor of her leadership and service.

Sister Mary Brigh was included in "Who's Who in America" and received many local, state, and national awards—her most treasured being the Benemerenti Medal conferred in 1971 by Pope Paul VI in recognition of her exceptional accomplishments and services.

Everyone knew Sister Mary Brigh Cassidy as a hospital administrator and a religious sister. Her close friends and colleagues knew that she wrote poetry.

Sister Mary Brigh Cassidy, 1980

Poems

Advent and Christmas

O Emmanuel
Our King and law-giver,
The expected of nations
And their Savior,
Come to save us
O Lord our God.

O Emmanuel is a profound act of adoration and an appeal of mankind at the throne of God. It begins with the name of Christ which was revealed to Isaiah and was heard when the angel spoke to Joseph ... We appeal to Him to come as our law-giver and king, and in the petition is the pledge that we will obey and be loyal.

Expectation

She waits her hour
With quiet eagerness—
Though this is joy beyond all understanding:
To carry close within her virgin breast
Her Son, yet sweeter will it be
To gaze adoringly upon His face,
To lose herself within those eyes,
So fathomless, so like her own,
And know they are the eyes of God.
To cradle in her arms her Babe
Whose tiny hand holds countless worlds and suns.
To lull to rest Him Whose rest is eternity.

12•1937

First Christmas

When Lady Mary knelt to pray
Beside her small Son's bed,
The little cherubs gathered close
To hear the words she said.

They listened with angelic care
To catch her every word,
For hers would be the loveliest prayer
That heaven ever heard.

They watched with breathless ecstasy
Her smile of tender bliss,
As she gently soothed her Babe and pressed
His small hand with a kiss.

Their whispering wings they folded close
And listened all night long,
While the silent words of the Lady's prayer
Filled heaven and earth with song.
By the side of her Son, so helpless and small,
And knew Him, Lord and the Master of all.

Near ears that will never fail to hear
The song of the angels, mystic but clear
And the silken whisper of silver wings
At the awesome moment when Christ the King
Is reborn in the Christ-Mass Mystery,
And Bethlehem merges with Calvary.

And lastly come Magi-hands that can hold
The heaped up wealth of your heart and soul,
All of the people and things that you love,
All of earth below and Heaven above,
Only to lay them all at the feet
Of a wondrous Babe Who slumbers sweet
While bright stars stand sentinel high above
And His Mother murmurs her song of love.

12•1946

Song
of
the Littler Angels

While great angels sing on high
          Gloria!

                   Gloria!

Echoing through the starlit sky
                        Gloria!

          Gloria!

Littler angels close at hand
Help unfold each swaddling band;
Try to warm the tiny feet
Of the new-born Infant sweet;
Lightly fluff His strawy bed
Murmuring softly round His head:

Baby Jesus, sleep a while,
Make Your lovely Mother smile,
She is weary, let her rest,
We will do our very best.
We, Your little angels, keep
Watch, so sleep, sweet Jesus, sleep.

12•1945

Christmas Crib

Flawless and clear as a precious gem
Hung the Christmas star in the eastern sky,
And wisemen followed, as wise men do,
The light of the star till it led them to
The Child Who was God most high.

Flawless and clear on each Christmas eve
Hangs the star of faith in life's midnight skies
And wise men follow its mystic rays
Till they lead to a place where a mother prays
By the crib where her Infant lies.

The crib may be ivory, paper or straw,
The figures stately, tawdry or small,
But humble men who are wise and kind
Though they kneel by the lowliest crib will find
The Infant Savior of all.

12•1947

Christmas Wishes

The glowing Christmas candles
Burn with a steady light,
And bells peal out a carol
Into the winter night.

For Christ the Infant Savior
Is born—the heavens rejoice,
And to that wondrous music,
Man adds inspired voice.

May the glad joy of Christmas
Be of your life a part,
And Christmas lights keep shining
Forever in your heart.

11•1933

Epiphany

In darkness grope the peoples of the world,
The light of truth has faded in the gloom,
And shadow seekers are the men who try
To trace it to its source, there is no room
For ought but sadness or a dull despair.

A sign, O Lord, Thy people ask a sign!
Thou Who has led them in the days of old

Out of captivity into the light of the day,
Let not Thy children into slavery be sold,
But in Thy mercy grant a sign that all may share.

A new star in the heavens brightly shines,
And leads three wise men on their perilous way.
From distant lands to Bethlehem, where they find
A new-born infant in the manger laid,
And at the Child—God's feet their gifts they leave.

A cloudless day and on the Jordan's banks,
John, who has come to make way for the king,
Baptizes in His name, the multitude
And with them Mary's Son, a loud voice rings,
"This is My Divine Son, in whom I am well pleased."

A marriage feast, and at His Mother's word,
A half grown Boy turns water into wine,
The first of many miracles which prove
That Mary's Son most truly is divine,
That at His touch all pain and want will cease.

Nor will He fail the world in its dark hour,
When faith and hope are at their lowest tide,
When charity has all but ebbed away;
Instead He draws yet nearer to our side
To bring the blessing of abiding peace.

1•1936

Gifts of the Spirit

What gifts shall I give this Christmas? Your answer depends upon the answer to another question. Why do I give Christmas gifts? The answer leads us back nineteen hundred and forty-four years to a little hamlet in Judea. There in a setting of stark poverty, a broken manger in a cold, dark stable, we find a maiden mother kneeling beside the first Christmas Gift, the Infant Jesus.

That first Christmas set a precedent that should never be abandoned. Every true Christmas gift must include the giver, just as God gave Himself when He sent His Divine Son to bring peace and happiness to the world.

But how can I give myself? Can I wrap myself in gay tissues tied with ribbon and holly to be placed beneath a shining tree? You can, but it is not necessary. You give yourself most effectively through your kindness, your courtesy, and your friendly helpfulness.

It is Christmas Eve. You step off a crowded bus in the falling snow. A wispy little woman you have never seen before drops an unwieldy bundle. You stoop quickly, pick it up, and restore it to her with a cheery greeting. Her eyes light up with pleasure. A Christmas gift has been given.

The tree is lighted in the corner of the living room. The dinner table is set for Christmas Eve. There are tall, red candles on the buffet, holly on the curtains, and the spicy odor of good food is floating in from the kitchen. You slip out of your coat and say, "Isn't it good to be at home!" Your mother smiles, your little brothers push each other and upset the footstool, the dog rubs his nose against your ankle. A Christmas gift has been given.

It is five o'clock Christmas morning. You are blinking in the bright light of the church after a quick walk through the icy starlight. There is silence, broken only by muted footsteps. Then the lights glow brighter and the organ floods the church with the glorious music of Christmas. It brings back all of the Christmases you have ever known. In a moment the faces of all those you love pass before you and become a part of the joy in your heart and your prayer for their safety and happiness. A Christmas gift has been given.

Back home again your little sister is eager to display her culinary skill. You really don't want an egg for breakfast, but when she says eagerly, "Let me fix you one specially," you smile and say, "I'd love it." Ten minutes later she produces a slightly lopsided egg with the triumph of an artist. A Christmas gift has been given.

Still later, the telephone rings. They are sorry but some one is ill. Could you help out for a few hours? Your eyes travel briefly over the bright happy room, you hesitate a moment, and then you say, "Of course I will help. Merry Christmas!"

12•1944

Another Mary

Mary, being three,

Doesn't really see
Why the Baby Jesus should be lying in the cold.

Mary wants to know

If she may not go
To find her woolly sweater
and warm Him from the cold.

Mary's eyes are wide

As we kneel beside
The crib of Baby Jesus, and I tell her why He came.

Mary's eyes are dew,

Lips a tremble too
As she says,
"I love Him but let's warm Him just the same."

12•1944

I love Him

Nazareth

Remember
How short Christ's hour on Tabor.
Even Bethlehem and Calvary
Are brief in span when placed beside
The quiet years at Nazareth.
Years of little things:
Rising and lighting fire and drawing clear
Cool water at the well; watching each day
Sunrise and sunset, flowers bloom and fade.
Years of humble tasks, of honest toil,
Of grateful rest at eve, of quiet nights
Unstirred by troubled rumors, blessed by prayer.

All other places on this earth
Knew Him by days or months;
Nazareth can count the years.
Well was He called Jesus of Nazareth,
Well the stark inscription on the cross
Contained that lowly name, Nazareth:
Symbol of simple lives and gracious ways,
Of love and toil, peace and fidelity.
Haven of family life, first Christian home,
Where Mary, Queen of Mothers, served her own.

3•1943

Lent and Easter

After the Sabbath, at dawn on the first day of the week, Mary Magdalene and the other Mary went to look at the tomb. 2 There was a violent earthquake, for an angel of the Lord came down from heaven and, going to the tomb, rolled back the stone and sat on it. 3 His appearance was like lightning, and His clothes were white as snow. 4 The guards were so afraid of Him that they shook and became like dead men. 5 The angel said to the women, "Do not be afraid, for I know that you are looking for Jesus, who was crucified. 6 He is not here; He has risen; just as He said. Come and see the place where He lay. 7 Then go quickly and tell His disciples; 'He has risen from the dead and is going ahead of you into Galilee. There you will see Him'. Now I have told you."

MATTHEW 28: 1–7

Mother of Sorrows

How often His baby head was pressed
Against your mother's breast,
And in the way that mothers have
You lulled your Son to rest.

But even then your tender heart
Knew more of grief than joy,
You know what sin would one day do
To Him, your God, your Boy.

Now once again that head is pressed
Against your mother's breast,
But now 'tis still in death and leaves
Dark blood stains where it rests.

The thorns that pierced His gentle head,
The sword that pierced His Heart,
Now find a second lodging place
Deep in your anguished heart.

Each drove the nails yet deeper in
The quivering flesh of One,
Who holds the Heavens in His hand,
But spared not His own Son.
For thus 'twas prophesied of old,
And even thus 'twas done.

In darkness, pain, and agony
The Boy who played at Mary's knee
Paid freely, uncomplainingly

The ransom of all men.
Loosed as a God alone could loose
The fetters forged by sin.

7•1936

Crucifixion

A bleak hill and a rocky hill,
We climb with lagging tread;
Low darkening skies and thunderbolts.
Have filled us with vague dread;
And spring that was so close below,
Seems here forever fled.

'Twas such a day on such a hill,
He hung between Earth and Sky;
The Savior of the Universe,
The very God of Heaven and Earth,
And in agony did die.

Not for a wrong that He had done,
Perfection cannot sin;
But for the sins of men long dead,
And uncreated men;
And every sin stood separately,
As if it then had been.

 1935

Not for a wrong that
He had done

Easter

Awake to the glory that Easter brings,
Lift your face to the rising sun and sing

        Allcluia!

Share with the holy women of old
The wondrous message the angels told,

      Alleluia!

The April air is fragrant and clean
And the swelling buds wear a glint of green,
While the dormant life in the dullest cloud
Stirs at the quickening touch of God,

      Alleluia!

Life, new life, when the old is spent,
Life triumphant, a sacrament,
Life eternal succeeds the gloom
Of the withered seed, of the empty tomb,

        Alleluia!

4•1944

Ordinary Time

This season does not get the attention and focus that the seasons of Lent or Advent do—nor are we as familiar with the term Ordinary Time—a time when nothing seems to be expected, yet so much of life happens in the day-to-day activities of our lives. It is found in the summertime here in Minnesota, as people try to live a little differently, spend time in a little less structured way, and, of course, enjoy the great outdoors.

What does this Ordinary Time mean to each one of us? What are the unnoticed aspects of our lives? What extraordinary events are occurring, possibly in ways so familiar they do not seem important today? Looking back, we each can recall and remember people and places that have had an impact on our lives because somehow they have changed us. Our greatest moments of change occur in ordinary daily events of birth, life, and death, and in the day-to-day routine of living, working, and caring about family, friends, and leisure.

This is how our faith life grows. Over time, with confidence in God present in our life, we build the Kingdom spoken of in the Gospel. In our lives, we are planting what we hope are good seeds of wheat. In our own ordinary way, we are invited to help build the Kingdom day after day in the manner in which we have been given the skill. No more or less is asked of us.

—Sister Kate Manahan, O.S.F.

If I Have Come

If I have come to Thee alone in sorrow,
And in joy forgot that Thou art God;
If I have only sought for favors from Thee,
Never bringing hymns of simple praise,
I stand convicted.

Come to Me ye who labor

- yes, but not alone

When you are laboring, come too when you play;

Come to Me when ye mourn

- yes then, but come

When you have comfort found and are rejoicing.

Poor is the faith and poorer still the love
Of him who asks, receives, and goes upon his way
Forgetting Him who gave, oh let not this
Be mine, Oh Lord, but ever let me come
To Thee, whatever day or hour may bring.

10•1935

Harvest Moon

The harvest moon is full,
Its beams are long and red:
Is the corn all shocked?
Will the cattle all be fed?

The harvest moon is full,
It gives a golden light;
Are the barns and bins full?
Will we stand the winter right?

The harvest moon is full,
There's a shadow on its face;
Have we failed in our part?
Have we lost in the race?

The harvest moon is full,
Work and labor had its day;
Now the toiler rests in peace,
Now at last he has his pay.

The harvest moon is full,
Let us dance and happy be,
Thank the God of the Harvest
For the plenty that we see.

10•1935

On a Leaf Falling

It gently brushed against my cheek,
Then fell discarded to the street,
To meet alike the rumpling of
The autumn wind and restless feet.

Discarded? No, in God's great plan,
Matter and man alike are brief,
And yet He does not fail to note
The falling of each withered leaf.

10•1935

Autumn

There's magic afoot every night in the fall,
And at daybreak we find with delight,
That an Artist of marvelous talent has touched
The world with His brush overnight.

There's a great splash of red in the oak tree,
Bright yellow's the maple's gay hue,
And barberry bush in the border
Is flaming with scarlet anew.

He works against time, this great artist,
Nothing short of perfection will do,

For too soon turns the page, leaving but memories
To last us the long winter through.

10•1935

Full Moon

The full moon tonight
Is a very pale gold,
Like the shade of winter sun
On a tiny baby's hair.

The shadow on the moon
Is a brooding angel,
Wings half-furled
Head bowed down, face veiled.

We have hoped long for rain,
There's a promise of it there;
Oh for the sting of bright drops on the cheek,
And the fragrance of rain in the air!

1931

Paradox

They who are overlong in learning
How little are small things,
Are overlong too, in discerning
Greatness in little things!

2•1939

An Ideal

Many a verse is written,
And many a poem read,
With never a thought of the singing words
That never have quite been said.

We build us a poem of fancy,
Or one of reality;
We touch on life at its beginning,
We touch on eternity.

But often when words are the fairest,
And phrases are coupled and rhyme,
Until they sound to thc flattered ear
Like a mellow, much-loved chime.

How often 'tis only an echo
Of the thought that gave it birth;

And the poet turns frustrated
To interests of little worth.

1929

This is Autumn

Sumac flings a scarlet challenge
From the hilltop to the sky,
Maples, clad in flaming armor
March in stately columns by.

Prim backyards and gracious gardens
Share alike a wealth untold—
Shaggy headed purple asters,
Dahlia, russet, marigold.

Busy squirrels, their sleek jowls bulging,
Vie for soundest nuts to store;
Crickets strum their elfin fiddles
Every night outside my door.

Dry leaves murmur at the advent
Of each breeze and passer-by
While wreath like threads of fragrant wood smoke
Trace ghost pictures in the sky.

10•1944

Noblesse Oblige

He to Whose service I am pledged
Is King of glory, King of earth;
Then I, His bride, must also be
A queen of noble birth.

O Christ, my King, I little know
The etiquette of royalty.
But this I know, a true queen is
Unfaltering in loyalty.

So though Your footsteps lead me on
Dark pathways and Your service bring
Battles and scars, I'll falter not
But follow to the end, my King.

10•1936

Thanksgiving

Life holds so very many beautiful things—
Laughter and tears,
Days of hard work and the quiet that evening brings,
Strength forged from fears.

Freedom to choose from the world's broad highways
The road we trod;
Home, loved ones, friends who support us always,
Staunch faith in God.

A multitude of taken-for-granted blessings,
Sunshine and rain,
A bird in flight, a song, a rose new-blooming,
Fields of ripe grain.

Life holds so very many wonderful blessings,
Thank God for them all;
From the rising sun,
                    through noon-day
                                and on to life's ending,
Thank God for them all.

11•1946

Thanksgiving

Thanksgiving means the giving of thanks,
The expression of gratitude;
The recognition that
                    we cannot make
                    all of our own happiness,

That others have contributed to it,
Not because they were obliged to
But because they wished to help us.

                    Gratitude—
            the response to the friendly smile,
The reward for the small favor sought and granted,
Or for the greater favor, unsought and yet received.

                    Gratitude—
            for the things we know are for our good,
And for the unsuspected good we may one day recognize.

                    Gratitude—
            for a helping hand in a simple need,
Or for powerful support in an hour of crises.

                    Gratitude—
            that leads us through appreciation
                    of the goodness of men,
To a higher appreciation of the goodness of God.

Thanksgiving means the giving of thanks,
The expression of gratitude.

11•1947

Thanksgiving

"Thank you" comes naturally when children pray
For children know that they are very small,
And that the world surrounding them is all
The work of others — parents, teachers, God.

"Thank you" comes naturally when children pray
For children see life with untroubled eyes,
No wonder really takes them by surprise
For all is wonderful, and good, and true.

Grant to us grace, dear Lord, to be
Your children always, make us see
However great our work, or small,
Your gracious power supports it all.
Teach us to thank You every day
As children thank You, when they pray.

11•1951

Teach Me

Teach, Lord, this busy brain of mine to find
Unfathomed riches in the thought of Thee.
Teach, Lord these restless hands of mine to find
Unending service in their work for Thee.
Teach, Lord these stumbling feet of mine to find
The narrow path that ever leads to Thee.
Oh teach this seeking soul of mine to find
Repose and peace in union close with Thee.
And teach this eager heart of mine to find
Fulfillment of its every need in Thee.
And teach this wayward will to lose itself
Forever in abandonment to Thee.

12•1936

Earth's Prodigality

Nothing that I have ever done
Could earn the privilege for me
Of witnessing anew each year
Grccn springing grass, fresh budding tree.

No dreams I e'er might dream could bring
This clear still blueness to the sky,
Or send that fluff of downy clouds
Sailing in lazy squadrons by.

Yet mine is the warm breath of spring
That perfumes every gentle breeze,
The song of lark, the glow of flower,
For Earth is prodigal in these.

4•1936

Our Shrine

Each night I see her shining through the darkness,
A gracious sentinel she stands on guard,
At once our inspiration and protection—
Our Lady of the Corner of the Yard.

From the window she is but a graceful outline,
Illuminated in a shrine of golden light,
But my memory reconstructs each gentle feature,
Her smile, her tenderness, with all her might.

Our home is thronged with figures of our Lady—
Our chapel, classrooms, corridors she guards,
But none awakens higher, stronger courage,
Than our Lady in the Corner of the Yard.

1•1937

Marble Halls

Man made these marble temples!
Yes, in a sense, man made.
Man drew the plans, welded the girders, laid the heavy beams.
But whose mind planned the shining marble, set the gleams
Of vanished sunsets in it, built it strong and tall
Enough to form the massive pillars and the lofty walls?
Whose artistry traced skillfully the myriad patterned veins
Of color, soft as those in old cathedral window panes?
Man made these marble temples!
Yes, in a sense, man made.
Man made these marble temples
From marble God had made.

8•1942

Magnificat

My soul doth magnify the Lord
 Who called me all unbidden in my youth
 To be His own, Who led me in His way;
 Who placed within my mind the light of truth,
 Who taught my heedless heart to love and pray.

❧

 Who blessed my slightest efforts with His Grace;
 Who labored with me in the noon-day heat
 Of life, Who marked each sacrifice,
 And sanctified each sorrow, made it sweet.

❧

 Who filled my heart with laughter, simple joy.
 My life with gracious friends, yet was alone
 My only Love, Who gave His dearest one
 On earth, His Virgin Mother, for my own.

❧

 Who, now that hours grow heavy and the weight
 Of years at times tempts me to beg release,
 In mercy bids me rest in Him and guides
 My slowing footsteps in the way of peace.
My soul doth magnify the Lord.

8•1942

Ode to Mary
on Her 20th Birthday

Through the dusty field she trudges
With her sprinkler lifted high,
Dealing death to bugs and such things,
If her arsenate they try.

Mary in blue gingham apron,
Smudgy cheek and socks rolled low,
In a tattered, broad brimmed sun hat,
Up and down the rows she goes.

Funny, for this is her birthday,
Twenty years she is today;
What a birthday party this is!
Mary, list to me, I say.

Why not trailing organdy?
Why no gay bandeaux?
Why no blithesome fluttering
As to a dance you go?

Mary, so the story tells,
Chose to go apart;
Mary, so it also tells,
Chose the better part.

7•1936

Vigil

Through the dark watches of the night we keep
A loving vigil by your silent bier,
And prayers we breathe to the Eternal God,
Who loved you greatly for you suffered much,
Are less a plea for mercy for your soul,
Than alleluias for your journey home.

So close in life you lived to death that now
Its reality is less real than the cloud,
That hovered o'er you long. Grief cannot be
The part of those who knew and loved your ways;
The sequel to life's night we know
You've found,
On the bright threshold of Eternal Day.

12•1935

Limerick

White hawthorne as fair as a bride and as graceful
Enfolds the brown road in warm intimacy,
The air holds the fragrance of dew and the soft kiss
Of winds carried in on grey mists from the sea.

Beyond brown bog and green field
                  the blue hills are beckoning.
Hasten, make haste, linger not by the way,
For the fairies dance here in the cool silver moonlight,
Each moment is magic in Ireland in May.

The music of church bells floats down from the hillside,
The small donkey pricks up long ears at the sound,
Not fairies, but angels have power to bestir him
And lift his meek eyes from the soft dusty ground.

Not a soul but ourselves is abroad this May morning
All Limerick is ours for the taking it seems,
Its peace and its friendliness stretch out around us
Clothed in a mantle of memories and dreams.

5•1952

Petition

Whatever change or routine my life brings,
Never, dear Lord, let me get used to things!

The crystal lace of snowflakes,
The purple mantled hills,
A widening silver crescent
Of moon, the starlight still.

The glory of the sunrise
Across the waters blue;
The saucy heads of tulips,
First violets, fresh with dew.

The crooning of a mother
Who lulls her son to sleep;
A toddler whose bedraggled doll
Makes her forget to weep.

Shoulders that sag, discouraged,
White faces etched by pain,
Tired eyes that will not open
Upon this world again.

White Host and burnished Chalice
Upraised in Sacrifice,
Each day, Divine fulfillment
Of love that can suffice.

Tune my heart, Lord, to every note life sings,
Lest I get used to any of Thy things.

2•1939

Sister Mary Joseph

Your heart was fashioned wide and deep and kind
That none might ever seek your aid in vain,
That mankind, bowed beneath its cross of pain,
In you might help a consolation find.
Your hands were fashioned small and deft and sure,
No strangers they to surgery's fine art,
Nor to skilled nursing where they played a part
Unrivaled, yet untouched by glory's lure.
Your soul was fashioned fine and strong and true.
How steadfastly you walked before the Lord
Seeking perfection, each act in accord
With Him Whose Will you ever sought to do.
Wise with the wisdom of simplicity,
For love of God you served humanity.

4•1939

Prelude to Prayer

Hydrangeas press their heavy coral heads
Against me as I pass along my way
To prayer, the cloister frames a willow tree
Whose branches, like a fairy fountain spray,
Ascend and fall in shimmering ecstasy.

Beyond stretch vistas shady, green and still,
Through which I glimpse the purple hills arrayed
In mantles intricately made of sunset skies,
And brilliant maple trees of countless shades,
But lately dipped in autumn's richest dyes.

Tonight the Office hymns are vibrant praise
Of Him Whose understanding Hand has led
Me down hydrangea-bordered paths and given
So much of beauty with my daily bread.

10•1938

*So much of beauty with
my daily bread*

Teresan Summer

Here I have known the peace of summer's day,
The soft, cool turf where shadows lightly fall,
The silence broken by the killdeer's call
And warblers singing an enchanted way.

 Here I have seen the poplar's shimmering leaves
Twinkle like fairies in an elfin dance,
And frisking squirrels fix their shining glance
On silver maples swaying in the breeze.

The lazy clouds drift slowly through the sky
And lose themselves behind the smoky hills,
And every earth-born creature softly trills
That heaven is near, no need to reason why.

7•1939

Heights

Each night let me climb a high hill
While the crimson sunset dies,
Painting bright with its glowing colors
The world which beneath me lies.

And if ever there be no high hill
For each evening's eager goal,
May I always find a high hill
Hidden deep in my secret soul.

7•1937

To a Memory

'Twere idle to attempt to phrase
The thoughts of which words cannot express;
Our sorrow at your going forth,
No words could e'er make less.

Unsparingly you spent yourself
To lift the load of death and pain;
Many who never knew your name,
New life through you have gained.

Now in the midst of service rare
You too have fallen in the fray,
And loving hand and skillful care,
Alike were powerless to say nay.

But in the places where you worked,
We seem to hear your quick step yet;
Your skill, your wisdom, your great heart,
No one who knew you could forget.

You leave a precious memory,
'Twill brightly shine for many a day,
For ideals of true service marked
Each step along your life's highway.

11•1935

You leave a precious memory

Night Prayer in a Hospital

Have pity, Lord, this night,
On all within these walls who toss in pain,
Be solace to their woes, may Thy still peace
Enfold them, quiet as the summer rain.

Have pity, Lord, this night,
On those whose hearts have wandered from Thy way,
Or never known the bounty of Thy love,
Be to them all a fire by night, a cloud by day.

Have pity, Lord, this night,
On all who will give up their souls to Thee.
Before another dawn, with heaven's court
May they adore Thee for eternity.

Have pity, Lord, this night,
On all who serve Thy suffering children's need,
Make skilled their hands, tender their hearts, that they,
Like Thee, may never crush the bruised reed.

8•1948

Silence

Silence can be a sinister thing:
The black silence of an unfriendly house
That a creaking stair-tread shatters like clattering glass.

Silence can be a dull weary thing:
The grey silence of a man slouching on a broken doorstep,
Too tired and hopeless for words.

Silence can be a cool tranquil thing:
The green silence of a sheltered garden
Where shadows fall lightly
and even the song of birds is muted.

Silence can be a still, hallowed thing:
The white silence of the golden tabernacle
Where Christ waits, unwearied
            for the coming of the sons of men.

4•1944

Campus in Spring

Red roofs, blue skies, green lawns, and purple hills,
Tall, slender, swaying trees, cardinals' trills,
Fragrance of lilacs, flash of golden wings,
Heart-breaking loveliness, campus in spring.

5•1936

Formality

It was a formal occasion,
And so we were formal.
I recited my carefully rehearsed request,
And you propounded your carefully prepared questions,
To which I gave the anticipated answers.
But all the time there was a friendly little gleam
In your eye, which said,
"I am not always this way.
Personally, I prefer unassuming simplicity,
But my office requires certain ceremonial forms,
And this is a formal occasion."
And so we were formal.

7•1936

Remembrance

Ever we found it gentle,
Your cool, restraining hand;
In all our darkest moments,
Sure you would understand.

Often 'twas only little things
That you would say or do,
But always they made us sharers of
Your Faith, so strong and true.

Forever you will be with us,
Whatever ways we trod;
Your fingerprints upon our hearts
Made them more truly God's.

6•1936

Forever you will be with us,
Whatever ways we trod

"His Ways Are Not Our Ways"

By His own will He came into the world
In poverty; He labored with his hands,
From Joseph, learned to build in a way.
Yet, He was God from whose Hand came the world,
A doubting world which could not understand
His ways are not our ways.

The Jewish people waiting for a king
To bring them wealth, and power, and victory;
To make of them God's chosen here on earth.
How could this dying prophet be a king,
This broken figure on the shameful tree?
Can Death to Life give birth?

A paradox? Yes, paradox it seems,
For 'twas the victor who met with defeat,
And He who died lives on through endless days;
'Tis light, not darkness, that from Calvary gleams
And brings a world suppliant to His feet,
His ways are not our ways!

5•1936

A Day

This fragile toy I hold within my hands,
An unspent day;
The distance from a dawn to even-tide;
A slender string of hours
That I may put to various use;
May drop them one by one,
Never to be recalled;
Or set them carefully,
Each bead a shining jewel in
The pattern of my life.

1•1936

Blizzard

Swirl snow and blow,
Descend to the earth in mad scamper,
Pause for a moment then tear on,
Blocking the pathways and highways,
Turning trees into silhouette crystals,
Charming dull slattern shacks into mansions;
Bringing surges of hot blood to cold cheeks,
Changing quick breath to frost on fur collars,
Hanging lashes with quivering diamonds.

Swirl snow and blow,
What though a medley of winters,
Has brought like adventures to others;
This is your day and yours only,
Sovereign dictator of winter.
Throw yourself madly against me,
With the force of an uncontrolled fury;
I too, have known other winters,
You have not power to confound me!

Swirl snow and blow
Something is rising within me,
Something that laughs at your antics,
Something that mocks at your fury,
Something that says "Come storm with me!"
I too, would join in your dancing,

In your mad senseless cavorting
Nor would I ever grow weary,
Never fail to rise fresh to your summons.

2•1936

Fragments

I bring you only trifles, broken fragments,
The little things that constitute my day,
The countless interruptions, irritations,
The hours when I work and rest and pray.

If it were something great that You required
With Your help I would bring it to You too,
But now it's simple little things You're asking,
So I must offer fragments, Lord, to You.

Trusting that when they're gathered all together,
The odds and ends that make this life of mine,
Your touch will weld them into one clear pattern
And find a place for them in heaven's design.

8•1937

Thine Was the Choice

Thine was the choice, O Lord, not mine.
Intent on other things I went
My careless way, and heeded not
The gentle call you sent.

You let me go—my way to try,
You waited for me through it all,
And then one day again you sent
Another, more insistent call.

No credit mine, that I have come!
Thy choice, not mine drew me apart.
Ah, grant, Dear Lord, that to life's end,
That call may echo in my heart.

12•1936

For Light

Grant I may never lose You, Lord, in crowded ways,
When things and people fill the busy days
With pressing needs and multiple demands,
Let not the surge of changing joys and fears,
The triumphs turned to bitterness and tears,
Lead me to think You do not understand.
When other ways seem safer help me see
This is Your choice, and so is best for me.

11•1940

A Tree

It is a gracious thing—a Tree,
Its graceful hands stretch out to me;
A lady fair of high estate,
With smiles alike for poor and great;
A lady fair of high degree,
It is a gracious thing—a Tree!

7•1928

Change

Change is inexorable,
It is change,
It is sometimes silent, the seed in the earth,
It is sometimes thunderous, the onslaught of the tempest,
It is sometimes raucous, the cheers of the mob,
It is change.

Change is inexorable,
It is change.
Enthusiasm may stimulate it,
Violence may force it.
Resistance may hinder it,
Analysis may clarify it,
Change is inexorable, it is change.

Change is a blessing,
Change is a curse,
Change is a builder,
Change is a destroyer.
Safe in the hands of no man,

Placed in the hands of all men,
The Word germinating in the dark earth.
Change is inexorable,
It is change.

1968

Content

Though I should fail a hundred times,
And like as not it's fail I will,
It's better so; should I attain
All that I seek and have my fill
Of happiness. I might some day
Come to believe I knew the way
To live!

 Failures are sharp and shining spurs
Urging me on to unknown heights
Where faith and hope will meet and merge
Lost in reality's clear light.
He who attains all his desires
Has warmed his hands at meager fires,
Not lived!

2•1939

Subterfuge

Whenever You cannot fill the emptiness of my heart,
It is because it is not empty at all,
But cluttered with plans, small loves, and sensitive pride;
When with foolish prudence I fail to throw open wide
The door and strip the chambers clean to the wall,
For fear of losing a little,
I risk the losing of all.

7•1939

Request

Give me my high moments
Even though I pay
With aching head and weary heart
For many a lonely day.

Give me life's full measure
Even though I tire;

Each cooling heap of smoldering ash
Was once a glowing fire.

Lurking in each shadow
There will ever be
The magic spark that constitutes
Reality for me.

2•1936

Concession

Since you insist,
Or to be more exact, imply quite courteously,
That stately ways and sober thoughts are best for me,
I will walk carefully not let my glances stray.
But ask not that my heart
Beat soberly for always it will race
Ahead, exploring fragrant paths of May.

5•1941

Vision

Lord, that I may see—
Each face, the vision of Thy own,
Each plea for help, a call from Thee,
Each broken plan, Thy wiser choice,
Each pain, Thy sorrow shared with me.

Each task, Thy Nazareth renewed
Each recompense, Thy hundredfold,
Each love, a quiet foretaste of
The treasure of Thy love untold.

8•1944

Blessing of Saint Francis

May the Lord bless thee and keep thee,
That thou mayest ever serve Him faithfully;
May He show thee His face,
Lest the darkness of despair encompass thee;
And have pity on thee,
When in thy weakness thou wanderest from fidelity;
May He turn His Face toward thee,
That in Its light all else may fade from thee;
And grant thee the peace
Of a heart wise in humility.

5•1936

One of many depictions of Saint Francis of Assisi on the Saint Marys campus

Notes

We can only speculate on Sister Mary Brigh's thoughts and reflections as she wrote her poetry. Her words are holy and often feel full of thanksgiving and gratitude. The poetry is rich in spiritual reflections. Sister wrote around the Liturgical Year of the Catholic Church. In like fashion, we organized this book according to the Liturgical calendar. We recognize some of the places and people she wrote about and have made some notes that the readers might use as they unwrap *the Gifts of Her Spirit!*

—Sister Lauren Weinandt, O.S.F.,
 and Jane K. Campion

- ◆ A copy of the "O" Antiphon, page 49, can be found in the window display of Saint Marys Hospital Chapel during the Advent season.

- ◆ "Gifts of the Spirit," page 56, was recorded in the *Saint Marys Hospital Bulletin* on December, 1944.

- ◆ "Another Mary," page 58, was based on a true incident. The little girl in the poem was the daughter of a patient who was in the hospital at Christmas time. One day while visiting her mother, the child was taken to the Chapel by one of the Sisters to see the Christmas crib. The child's reaction to seeing the statue of the Christ Child is recorded in the poem.

- The scriptural passage on page 61 can be found in the window display at Saint Marys Hospital Chapel during the Easter Season.

- The article on page 67 is by Sister Kate Manahan, O.S.F., who was a member of leadership of the Sisters of Saint Francis. It was published in *Connections* in 1996, the year Sister Kate died, and included in this book with permission from the Academy of Our Lady of Lourdes.

- "Our Shrine," page 80, is referring to the grotto of Our Lady of Lourdes in the northwest corner of the Convent of the Academy of Our Lady of Lourdes when it was located on Center Street NW in Rochester. The convent was closed in 1955 when the Sisters moved their home to Assisi Heights.

- "Magnificat," page 82, was written for Sister Anastasia's Diamond Jubilee.

- "Ode to Mary on Her 20th Birthday," page 83, may have been written for Sister Mary Brigh's biological sister, Mary.

- "Vigil," page 84—It was customary for the Sisters of Saint Francis to sit vigil during the night with Sisters who had died.

- "Limerick," page 85, was written while Sister Mary Brigh and Sister Pantaleon Navratil traveled to Ireland. Their trip was a gift from Mayo Clinic Doctors Philip S. Hench and Edward C. Kendall, who were Nobel Prize winners. The gift honored the scientific support given to their research by Sister Pantaleon.

- "Sister Mary Joseph," page 87, was penned the month of Sister Joseph's death. April 1939 must have been a very sad month for the Sisters.

- "To a Memory," page 91, recognizes Doctor E. Starr Judd who was one of the early surgeons at the Mayo Clinic.

- "Vision," page 105, was printed on Sister Mary Brigh's remembrance card at the time of her death in 1992.

- "Blessing of Saint Francis," page 106, is Sister Mary Brigh's personal version of the "Blessing of Saint Francis."

- The symbols used to mark sections of the book were inspired by images found at Saint Marys Hospital and Chapel.